The World of Mythology:
Chinese Mythology

By Jim Ollhoff

VISIT US AT
WWW.ABDOPUBLISHING.COM

Published by ABDO Publishing Company, 8000 West 78th Street, Suite 310, Edina, MN 55439. Copyright ©2011 by Abdo Consulting Group, Inc. International copyrights reserved in all countries. No part of this book may be reproduced in any form without written permission from the publisher. ABDO & Daughters™ is a trademark and logo of ABDO Publishing Company.

Printed in the United States of America, North Mankato, Minnesota.
112010
012012

♻ PRINTED ON RECYCLED PAPER

Editor: John Hamilton
Graphic Design: Sue Hamilton
Cover Design: Neil Klinepier
Cover Photo: Gonzalo Ordóñez
Interior Photos and Illustrations: AP-pg 6; Corbis-pgs 18, 20, 21, 22, 24, 25, 28 & 29; Getty Images-pg 23; Granger Collection-pgs 13, 16, 17, 26 & 27; iStockphoto-border image; NASA/GSFC/MITI/ERSDAC/JAROS, & US/Japan ASTER Science Team-pg 31; PhotoLibrary-pg 7; Thinkstock-pgs 5, 9, 11 & 19, Wikipedia-pgs 4, 8, 10 & 26.

Library of Congress Cataloging-in-Publication Data

Ollhoff, Jim, 1959-
  Chinese mythology / Jim Ollhoff.
    p. cm. -- (The world of mythology)
  ISBN 978-1-61714-718-0
  1. Mythology, Chinese--Juvenile literature. I. Title.
  BL1825.O45 2011
  398.20951--dc22

                    2010032582

CONTENTS

The Mighty Myth..4

China: An Ancient Civilization 6

Confucianism, Taoism, and Buddhism............................8

The Soul of Chinese Mythology.......................................12

Chinese Creation Stories..14

The Yellow Emperor 16

The Eight Immortals 18

Honoring Ancestors..20

Chinese Dragons...22

Reading the Future 24

Popular Gods and Goddesses...26

Glossary...30

Index 32

THE MIGHTY MYTH

The world is a big place. It is uncontrollable and unpredictable, and not always understandable. Sometimes bad things happen to good people, and we don't know why. Sometimes good things happen to bad people, and that makes us feel like life isn't fair. People of all places and all cultures throughout history have seen how difficult life can be.

One way that people deal with life's hardships is to tell stories. Stories can help us find meaning in difficult times. When something bad happens to us, we tell ourselves that the difficulty will make us stronger. We tell ourselves that we'll understand the meaning of it someday. We tell ourselves that it will all work out eventually. We tell ourselves that other people have experienced the very same hardships.

One ancient story popular in China was called the "mandate of heaven." It said that if a ruler was wise and compassionate, he would rule for a long

Emperor Kangxi ruled China for 61 years and was greatly honored.

time. If a ruler was selfish and stupid, the gods would soon remove him. This story, and others like it, helped people understand why things happened.

Stories help us cope with life. These stories are called myths. Myths are simply stories that tell us something important. Throughout history, myths have helped people make sense out of difficult situations. Myths help make life understandable.

Above: One way that people deal with life's hardships is to tell stories.

CHINA: AN ANCIENT CIVILIZATION

China is one of the oldest civilizations in the world. Pottery has been discovered that dates back to 8500 BC. Some Chinese villages along the Yellow River may have started as long ago as 7000 BC.

Chinese civilization probably began in areas along the Yellow River. However, villages, tribes, and communities soon sprang up all over China. By the early part of the Zhou Dynasty (1046–256 BC), unique Chinese culture and literature appeared. Over the years, several tribes and peoples became unified.

China had natural boundaries that limited its contact with the rest of the world. The giant Himalayan Mountains bordered China in the west. The forbidding Gobi Desert was in the north, and the Pacific Ocean lay to the south and east.

China is famous for the Great Wall. It was built as a defensive barrier against warring tribes of people from the north. The wall was once more than 3,000 miles (4,828 km) long. Large sections have been destroyed, rebuilt, or gone to ruin throughout the centuries. Leaders of the Qin Dynasty (221–207 BC) first began building the wall. By 600 AD, many parts were constructed, although much of the wall we see today goes back to the Ming Dynasty (1368–1644 AD).

Statues from the Qin Dynasty.

Above: The Great Wall of China once extended for more than 3,000 miles (4,828 km).

CONFUCIANISM, TAOISM, AND BUDDHISM

In ancient times, China contained many tribes and regions. Each region had unique gods and mythologies, including sky gods, sun gods, rain gods, and mythological stories to tell. These are often called Chinese folk religions.

But then along came Confucianism and Taoism. About the sixth century BC, a legendary man named Confucius, or Kong, began a way of thinking that became known as Confucianism. It is more of a philosophy than a religion, but it was very influential. It emphasizes the importance of being proper in one's actions. Stealing, greed, impoliteness, and other such

Above: Confucius, Lao Tzu, and a Buddhist arhat.

things are not proper or helpful. Loyalty to family, honoring others, and being caring and kind are traits that are valued in Confucianism.

Above: A portrait of Confucius, also known as Kong.

Above: According to legend, Taoism was started by Lao Tzu.

Taoism began about the same time as Confucianism. According to legend, Taoism was started by a man named Lao Tzu. He emphasized getting in touch with nature and the natural order of things. Lao Tzu said that if people can get in the flow, as nature gets in the flow, their lives will be a lot more peaceful.

Buddhism became very influential in China around 600 AD. It is a religion and philosophy based on the teachings of Siddhartha Gautama, a monk from ancient India. Buddhism stresses the importance of correct living in order to achieve a peaceful afterlife. Suffering in life, Buddhism says, is caused by a desire for material things.

After Confucianism and Taoism came along, ancient Chinese gods and myths didn't die out, but they changed. Chinese mythologies were retold through the philosophies of Confucianism and Taoism. For the Chinese, virtue and proper action became more important than trying to make the gods happy. In Chinese myths, the gods became polite and noble examples of how to live a good life. In the new mythologies, people who were very wise and helpful became gods (or immortals) themselves.

Above: Siddhartha Gautama's teachings are the foundation of the Buddhist religion.

The Soul of Chinese Mythology

Many cultures of the world were greatly influenced by their mythologies. However, that didn't happen as often in China. Perhaps because of China's vast size or early central governments, few national myths developed, such as were common in Greece. A powerful priesthood never developed, such as in Central America. While Egypt was full of how-to guides for the afterlife, China had few such guides. The Chinese had many gods, but the myths are often about human creativity and wisdom instead of gods directing human affairs.

In many cultures, the gods are often mischievous. They sometimes do evil things. Greek gods kidnapped people. Aztec gods drank human blood. Egyptian gods battled with each other. However, the Chinese gods were polite and well behaved. This might be because of the influence of Confucianism on Chinese culture.

Many Chinese myths tell of creative and wise people who are granted immortality as a reward for their contributions to society. Fu Hsi taught people how to fish and forge metal. Yu taught people how to stop dangerous river flooding. Shang Di invented clothing and coins. Shen Nong made medicine for people.

Above: Fu Hsi was said to have taught people how to fish and forge metal.

Above: Yu taught people how to stop dangerous river flooding.

Chinese Creation Stories

Chinese mythology has a few creation myths. The story of Pan Ku and the cosmic egg is a popular myth. Pan Ku was a god who looked like a hairy human with horns. He was locked up in a giant egg for a long time. Finally, when the egg broke open, Pan Ku emerged. The lighter parts of the egg floated up and became heaven. The heavier parts of the egg became the Earth. Pan Ku was afraid that the sky would fall to the Earth, so he held up the sky. He kept pushing on the sky, keeping it away from the Earth for 18,000 years.

After working for all that time, Pan Ku became exhausted. He fell down and died. His body became part of the Earth. His blood became the rivers and lakes. His breath became the wind. One of his eyes became the sun and the other eye became the moon. His hair became the grass, and his bones became the rocks. And the fleas on his body became the humans.

Right: When Pan Ku died, his body became part of the Earth.

Above: According to Chinese mythology, Pan Ku was afraid that the sky would fall to Earth, so he held it up for 18,000 years.

THE YELLOW EMPEROR

One popular Chinese myth is about Huang Di, who is also called the Yellow Emperor. Huang Di was a remarkable man. According to the myth, he was an emperor of China around 2700 BC. He created the first wheel and the first boats. He gave music and handwriting to the people of the world. He taught people how to make the first pottery. He taught people how to plant crops. In some myths, he even chased away dangerous wild animals.

Huang Di was a peace-loving warrior who sometimes had to defend the world from evil people or evil gods. The mountain god gave Huang Di a pill that granted immortality. He was so wise and helped so many people that he was made chief of all the gods. His wife, Lei Zu, brought silk to humanity.

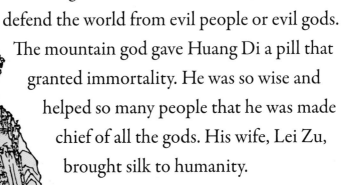

Left: Lei Zu, Chinese empress of Huang Di, stands beside trays of silkworms. The empress is credited by the Chinese with the invention of the loom and silk. According to legend, she discovered silk when a cocoon dropped into her teacup.

Above: According to Chinese mythology, Huang Di, also known as the Yellow Emperor, created the first wheel and the first boats. He gave music, handwriting, and pottery to the people. He was so wise and helped so many people that he was made chief of all gods.

THE EIGHT IMMORTALS

The Eight Immortals were six men and two women who achieved immortality by following Taoism very closely. Each of them had a special power, and looked after a special group of people. They continue to be popular characters in Chinese art and literature.

The Eight Immortals included Han Chung-li, who could turn metals into silver. He was the patron deity, or god, of the military. The Immortal known as Iron-Crutch Li was the patron deity of the sick.

Above: The Eight Immortals were six men and two women who achieved immortality by following Taoism very closely.

Another Immortal was Lan Ts'ai-ho, who represents the poor. She took care of a sick beggar and was rewarded with eternal life. Although usually presented as a woman, the myth stories differ on whether she was male or female.

According to myth, the Eight Immortals lived on a mystical island where there was no winter and no pain, and the rice bowls were always full.

HONORING ANCESTORS

It was common to honor ancestors in ancient China. One of the important parts of Confucianism is to be loyal to your parents. The idea is to continue to honor them and be devoted to them, even after they are dead. The Chinese didn't really worship their ancestors. They honored them. This was often called *venerating* their ancestors.

It was common to set up a small altar for dead parents or grandparents. Survivors would cook their ancestors' favorite food or pray to them. Sometimes survivors would lay pretend money on the altar as a way to make sure the ancestors were taken care of in the afterlife. They didn't believe their ancestors were gods. However, the ancestors took an interest in those who were still living, and the ancestors had the power to influence things in life.

Even today, in many parts of rural China, veneration of ancestors is still practiced the way it has been done for hundreds of years.

Right: A Chinese family worship their ancestors at a shrine in their home in the early 1900s.

Above: Framed pictures of ancestors form a shrine on a street in Guangzhou, China. Today, in many parts of China, veneration of ancestors is still practiced the way it has been done for hundreds of years.

CHINESE DRAGONS

In European mythology, dragons were fierce, evil creatures that were slain by brave knights. In Chinese mythology, dragons are almost never evil. In fact, they are usually a good luck charm, a sign of success or coming wealth.

Usually pictured as long, snake-like creatures with four legs, dragons probably were originally ancient rain gods. They were thought to live by the water, in lakes or rivers. They could fly, even though they are usually pictured without wings. Sometimes they are pictured in the clouds, since they were responsible for rain. Ancient Chinese villages often prayed to the dragons during times of drought. "Dragon dances" are still performed today at many Chinese New Year celebrations.

Chinese dragons were very powerful and frightening, but they usually used their power to protect people. There are many stories about dragons in Chinese mythology, and modern Chinese people still use the symbol of the dragon to represent authority and power.

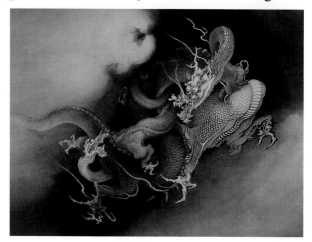

Right: Chinese dragons used their power to protect people.

Above: Dancers preparing for the Dragon Dance during the Chinese New Year in Hong Kong, China.

READING THE FUTURE

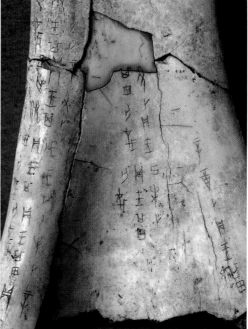

Above: An ancient Chinese oracle bone with questions written on it.

According to Chinese mythology, the universe is full of opposites—dark and light, peaceful and aggressive, cold and hot, female and male. There is always positive and negative energy present. These are called the yin and the yang. These opposites must be in constant harmony. If the harmony of the opposites is lost, then chaos is the result.

In many Chinese myths, people are able to tap into the energies of the universe to accomplish great feats, like magic or reading the future.

One popular way to read the future, also called divination, was by reading oracle bones. These were small animal bones, which were often sold as "dragon bones." A seeker would ask a question, and then the oracle bones would be heated until they cracked. A priest could then read the oracle bones and give the seeker an answer.

Originally, a book called the *I Ching* was also used for divination. A seeker would come with a question. A priest would throw special coins in the air and then check a passage in the *I Ching* for the answer to the question. Later, the *I Ching* became a book of philosophy.

Above: Coins were thrown by a priest, who then checked the *I Ching* for the answer to a question.

POPULAR GODS AND GODDESSES

For thousands of years, Chinese mythology and folklore has told the stories of hundreds of gods and goddesses, as well as many "immortals." These deities are celebrated for their virtues, their bravery, or for assisting common people.

Pan Ku: The creator god, child of parents yin and yang. He burst forth from the cosmic egg to construct heaven and Earth.

Huang Di: Also known as the Yellow Emperor, he was a mythical king who brought civilization to China.

Fu Hsi: An emperor sometimes called the Father of China. He is said to have created laws, writing, and the calendar. He was given immortality. Another creation story centers around Fu Hsi's wife, Nu Wa. This powerful goddess created people out of balls of mud, and later taught people how to raise children.

Jade Emperor: Sometimes called Shang Di or Yu Huang, this emperor invented many things for humanity, giving up his riches to help people. He was given immortality as a reward. His wife, Xi Wang Mu, looked out for women, especially those who were giving birth. She held a magic elixir that gave people immortality.

Yu: Another legendary leader of China. He was an engineer who built a system of canals that permanently controlled annual flooding. He was rewarded by becoming the next emperor, and then given immortality.

Yi: This ancient Chinese hero god was a great archer. At the beginning of the world, there were 10 suns in the sky. This made the world far too hot, and the crops withered. Yi took his bow and arrow and shot down nine of the suns so that the world could be a livable place. Yi's wife was named Chang-O. She was beautiful, but too curious. One day, she accidentally found the elixir of life. She drank it so that she could have immortality. She flew to the moon to become the moon goddess. One version of the myth says that the gods turned her into a toad to punish her for drinking the elixir of immortality. Her husband Yi visits her occasionally on the moon, which is why the moon is full and beautiful.

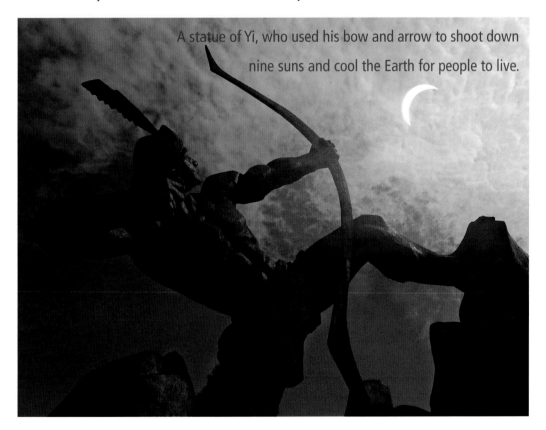

A statue of Yi, who used his bow and arrow to shoot down nine suns and cool the Earth for people to live.

GLOSSARY

BUDDHISM

A religion emphasizing living life without material desires so that there will be peace after death.

CONFUCIANISM

An important philosophy in China, emphasizing good works and loyalty in relationships.

DIVINATION

A way to read the future.

DYNASTY

The hereditary line of rulers of a country, such as the Han Dynasty. In China, periods of ancient history are usually measured in dynasties, instead of centuries, like in the West.

GREAT WALL OF CHINA

A tall, strong wall built to protect China from invaders. Leaders of the Qin Dynasty (221–207 BC) first began building the wall. The construction continued for about 1,000 years. The wall was once more than 3,000 miles (4,828 km) long, running across northern China. Today, it is about half that length. Large sections have been destroyed or gone to ruin throughout the centuries.

IMMORTALS

People or beings who never die.

SILK

A strong, soft, shiny fabric made from silkworm cocoons. Chinese Empress Lei Zu is credited with the invention of silk.

TAOISM

A philosophy of getting in touch with nature and the natural order of things.

YIN AND YANG

The harmony of opposites. The Chinese symbol is:

Above: A photo of a portion of the Great Wall of China taken from space in May 2001.

INDEX

B

Buddhism 10

C

Central America 12
Chang-O 29
China 4, 6, 8, 10, 12, 16,
　20, 26, 28
Confucianism 8, 10, 12,
　20
Confucius 8
cosmic egg 14, 26

D

divination 24
dragon bones 24
Dragon dance 22

E

Egypt 12
elixir of life 29

F

Father of China 27
Fu Hsi 12, 27

G

Gautama, Siddhartha 10
Gobi Desert 6
Great Wall of China 6
Greece 12

H

Han Chung-li 18
Himalayan Mountains 6
Huang Di 16, 26

I

I Ching 24
Immortals, Eight 18, 19
India 10
Iron-Crutch Li 18

J

Jade Emperor 27

K

Kong 8

L

Lan Ts'ai-ho 19
Lao Tzu 10
Lei Zu 16

M

mandate of heaven 4
Ming Dynasty 6

N

New Year, Chinese 22
Nu Wa 27

O

oracle bones 24

P

Pacific Ocean 6
Pan Ku 14, 26

Q

Qin Dynasty 6

S

Shang Di 12, 27
Shen Nong 12

T

Taoism 8, 10, 18

V

venerating ancestors 20

X

Xi Wang Mu 27

Y

yang 24, 26
Yellow Emperor 16, 26
Yellow River 6
Yi 29
yin 24, 26
Yu 12, 28
Yu Huang 27

Z

Zhou Dynasty 6